MEN'S DEVOTIONAL FOR DADS

5-Minute Devotions To Grow In Your Faith, Build Close Family Bonds, And Become The Parent Your Kids Need

Fox Bland

Copyright © 2024 by Biblical Teachings – All rights reserved

The content contained within this book may not be reproduced, duplicated, or transmitted without direct written permission from the author or the publisher.

Under no circumstances will any blame or legal responsibility be held against the publisher, or author, for any damages, reparation, or monetary loss due to the information contained within this book, either directly or indirectly.

Legal Notice:
This book is copyright-protected. It is only for personal use. You cannot amend, distribute, sell, use, quote, or paraphrase any part, or the content within this book, without the author or publisher's permission.

Disclaimer Notice:
Please note that the information contained within this document is for educational and entertainment purposes only. All effort has been executed to present accurate, up-to-date, reliable, and complete information. No warranties of any kind are declared or implied. Readers acknowledge that the author is not rendering legal, financial, medical, or professional advice. The content within this book has been derived from various sources. Please consult a licensed professional before attempting any techniques outlined in this book.

By reading this document, the reader agrees that under no circumstances is the author responsible for any losses, direct or indirect, that are incurred due to the use of the information in this document, including, but not limited to, errors, omissions, or inaccuracies.

TABLE OF CONTENTS

Leading the Flock at Home...4

Give Yourself a Pat on the Back..6

Real Men Change Diapers..8

Dealing With Overwhelming Stress.....................................10

Buddy Check..12

Chatting with the Big Guy Upstairs....................................14

Faith In The Fog...16

No 'I' in Parent...18

"Letting Them Fall to Fly": Watching them learn from life's little stumbles..20

Lessons, Not Lectures..24

The Unfinished Dad..26

The Art of the Apology...28

Tech, Trends, and Traditions..30

Dad's Time-Out..32

Counting Blessings, Not Problems....................................34

The Grateful Dad..36

Juggling the Daily Grind & Dad Duties..............................38

Recharging Dad's Batteries...40

The World through Their Eyes 44

More Than Just the Fun Dad 46

Teamwork Makes the Dream Work. 48

The Art of the Gentle No. 50

Fit Dad, Fun Dad 52

Penny-Wise Parenting. 54

Mental Fitness for Fathers 56

Tough Talks: Life, Loss, and Love 58

Make a Difference with Your Review 60

Guide, Don't Goad. 62

Training Wheels to Wings 64

Stand Up, Stand Out. 66

The Confidence Coach 68

Dad, the Peacekeeper. 70

Love Lessons at Home. 72

The Value of a Dollar 74

The Land of Nod 76

Self-Care Isn't Selfish 78

The 'Good Enough' Dad. 82

Chief Cheerleader & #1 Fan. 84

Birds and the Bees 86

The Family That Plays Together... 88

Walking the Dad walk 90

Fueling Their Fire... 92

Perfectly Imperfect Dad...................................... 94

Listening Ears, Speaking Hearts 96

Homework Helper and Life Coach 98

Dad's Diner: Teaching them to love foods that
love them back... 102

Solving the Puzzle of Parenthood........................... 104

Guardian Dad 106

Walking the Talk with the Good Book...................... 108

Moral Compass for the Modern Dad........................ 110

Doing It Right, Even When It Feels Wrong................. 112

Breaking the Dad Stereotypes 114

Stick With It, Dad... 116

Keep The Torch Alive 119

INTRODUCTION

"What time of day was Adam created? A little before Eve..."

Welcome, Dads, to a journey of self-discovery, growth, and inspiration. As you turn the pages of this devotional, you're stepping into a realm that honors your immense role – from daddy duty to grill master, and everything in between. Set forth on your year-long adventure, specially crafted to fit into the hustle and bustle of a dad's life. Whether you're working on your dad bod, hiding in your man cave, or busy fulfilling your role as papa bear, this devotional is your steadfast companion. It's designed to offer wisdom, laughter, and reflections that resonate with your unique fatherhood experience.

How to Use This Devotional

Each week brings a devotion that mirrors your daily life - the highs, the lows, and everything in between. These devotions are more than just words; they are echoes of the joys and challenges of your journey which is filled with punny dad jokes, super reflexes, and of course the love and strength you pour into your family. They're a tribute to your unique place in your family and in God's plan.

Short but impactful, each devotion is designed for the taxi dad's schedule while being rich in insights. As you read you'll find encouragement, practical advice, and a renewed sense of purpose in your calling as a dad. Embrace each week's lesson and step confidently into your God-given role – as a father figure and a beacon of guidance.

After reading the devotion, engage in your weekly 'Dad's Duty' task, reflect, and close with a prayer. Then, back to what you do best – being the 'old man' with a young heart, and the unsung hero of bedtime stories & bruised-knees.

This devotional is your companion, and a reminder that in every step of your fatherhood journey, you're not alone. Your role is pivotal, your struggles are acknowledged, and your victories are celebrated. Each devotion is a testament to your endless love and resilience as a dad.

Get ready, your journey begins now...

P.S. Your journey as a dad is unique, but you don't have to walk it alone. Scan the QR code below to join the 'Biblical Teachings' community on Facebook.

Stay connected, get inspired, and grow together.

LEADING THE FLOCK AT HOME

"Train up a child in the way he should go; even when he is old he will not depart from it."

– Proverbs 22:6

Have you ever wondered how to keep your children engaged and excited about faith? This was the puzzle Ethan, a father much like yourself, sought to solve. With three energetic children, Sunday church services often felt more like a routine than an enriching spiritual experience. Ethan longed to make faith a source of joy and inspiration in their lives.

Embracing this challenge, Ethan introduced "Faith Fridays." These evenings were dedicated to bringing Bible stories to life through interactive and fun activities. When the story of Noah was on deck, they built an ark from cardboard boxes, discussing trust and perseverance amidst life's challenges. The tale of David and Goliath transformed into a playful backyard slingshot contest, illustrating how courage and faith can topple giants.

Through these activities, Ethan's children began to see faith in a new light. The stories were no longer just words; they were experiences, lessons lived and laughed through. Ethan realized that his role as a spiritual leader was not only to guide but also to make the journey of faith an adventure, one filled with discovery and delight.

DAD'S DUTY

Reflect on how you can bring faith into your family life in a joyful and engaging way. Read a Bible story with your children and find a playful way to bring it to life. For older kids, you could discuss how a daily activity can reflect a biblical principle. Your task is to merge faith with fun in your home.

_____

_____

_____

_____

_____

_____

_____

_____

PRAYER

Dear God,

Empower me to lead my family with love, weaving Your teachings with joy, and making our faith journey a vibrant and joyful experience.

Amen.

GIVE YOURSELF A PAT ON THE BACK

2

"Well done, good and faithful servant."
— Matthew 25:21

Have you ever felt like your efforts as a father go unnoticed or unappreciated? You're not alone. Meet James, a father of two, who often felt his efforts were like seeds planted in a garden unseen. He worked tirelessly, providing, guiding, and loving, yet rarely did he stop to acknowledge his own achievements.

One evening, while reading bedtime stories to his children, his daughter whispered, "Daddy, you're my hero." Those simple words struck James deeply. He realized he had been so focused on being the perfect father that he hadn't taken a moment to appreciate the fruits of his labor. From the joy in his children's eyes, the warmth of their laughter, to the depth of their questions, James was succeeding in ways he hadn't stopped to recognize.

James learned an important lesson that night: acknowledging and celebrating the small victories in fatherhood is not just about self-congratulation; it's about recognizing God's work through him. Every bedtime story, every shared laugh, every lesson taught was a testament to his loving commitment as a father.

Like James, you too may not always see the immediate impact of your patience, your teachings, or the love you share. But rest assured, these moments are building blocks in your child's life. Every effort you make, big or small, shapes the world of your children, echoing the love and guidance of our Heavenly Father.

DAD'S DUTY

Reflect on the past week and identify moments where you made a positive impact on your children's lives, no matter how small. Give yourself credit for these wins, and write them down as a reminder that you're doing a great job. Share one of these moments with your family, letting them know how much it means to you.

_____

_____

_____

_____

PRAYER

Dear God,

Help me recognize the value in my efforts as a father, celebrating the small victories and Your guiding hand in my journey.

Amen.

REAL MEN CHANGE DIAPERS

3

"Whatever you do, work heartily, as for the Lord and not for men,"

– Colossians 3:23

Have you ever found yourself knee-deep in a situation you never imagined before fatherhood? Perhaps it was a task that felt beneath you, or just too messy? Picture Mark, a dad like many, who once believed that certain tasks were not 'manly' enough. The first time he faced the daunting task of changing his newborn daughter's diaper, he felt out of his depth, awkward, and hesitant. Yet, in that moment of messy discomfort, Mark experienced a profound change in perspective.

As he looked into his daughter's eyes, something shifted. He realized that every act of service for his child, no matter how small or unglamorous, was an act of love, a reflection of the servanthood Christ exemplifies. This mundane task was not just a duty; it was a privilege, an opportunity to demonstrate love in its purest form.

In embracing these moments, Mark discovered the true essence of strength and masculinity. It's not found in the avoidance of the messy or the mundane, but in the willingness to embrace every aspect of caring for another life. This is where real character and faith are shown.

DAD'S DUTY

Today, reflect on a task in fatherhood you usually avoid or find challenging. Approach this task with a new mindset, viewing it as a vital part of your service and love for your child. Recognize the strength and love demonstrated in these everyday acts of fatherhood.

_____

_____

_____

_____

_____

_____

_____

_____

_____

PRAYER

Dear God,

Help me embrace every part of fatherhood, finding joy and purpose in the humblest acts of care, as I serve You through loving my child.

Amen.

DEALING WITH OVERWHELMING STRESS 4

 *"Cast all your anxiety on him because he cares for you."*

– 1 Peter 5:7

Do you ever feel like you're juggling too many balls at once as a father? Financial pressures, family responsibilities, personal well-being – it can all feel like a towering stack ready to topple. Let's consider the story of Daniel, a father who found himself overwhelmed by the demands of life.

Daniel felt the weight of the world on his shoulders – a demanding job, financial strains, and the constant drive to be a good father and husband. He lay awake at night, his mind racing with worries. One evening, his daughter asked him to play, but he was too consumed by stress. Seeing the disappointment in her eyes was a wake-up call. Daniel realized he had let stress steal precious moments with his family.

He turned to prayer, not just for relief, but for guidance. Daniel started to prioritize, delegate, and most importantly, trust in God's plan. He learned to take each day as it came, focusing on what he could control and leaving the rest in God's hands. By doing so, he found peace amidst chaos, and the joy of fatherhood returned.

Like Daniel, you may be facing overwhelming stress. Remember, it's not about carrying the burden alone, but about finding strength in faith, and wisdom in simplicity and trust.

DAD'S DUTY

Reflect on what is currently causing you the most stress. Identify one step you can take today to alleviate this pressure. It could be as simple as delegating a task, spending quality time with your family, or setting aside time for prayer and reflection.

_____

_____

_____

_____

_____

_____

_____

PRAYER

Dear God,

Grant me peace amidst the chaos, clarity in the midst of challenges, and strength to transform my anxieties into positive actions.

Amen.

BUDDY CHECK

5

"As iron sharpens iron, so one person sharpens another."

– Proverbs 27:17

As you take on more responsibilities, it's easy for friendships to take a backseat. We've all been there, it's a common scenario once you step into the role of a dad. However, research suggests that strong social connections are crucial for our mental and emotional well-being. In fact, a study by Brigham Young University found that individuals with strong social relationships have a 50% increased likelihood of longevity compared to those who are lonelier.

As fathers, nurturing these friendships is not just beneficial for us, but it also sets a positive example for our children about the importance of relationships. It's about balance – managing your time and responsibilities so you can maintain your connections. Whether it's a regular check-in call, a catch-up over coffee, or a group chat, small efforts can keep these bonds strong. These friendships can provide not only joy or an outlet for relaxation and laughter, but also a support network, crucial for navigating the highs and lows of fatherhood.

Remember, you are your own person outside of your role as a dad. Try not to let fatherhood consume you to the point that you lose yourself. Monthly reminders to check in with friends can be all it takes to keep hold of that part of you.

DAD'S DUTY

Today, take a moment to reach out to a friend you haven't spoken to in a while. Send a text, make a call, or even plan a meet-up. Keep the lines of communication open. Maintaining friendships is vital for your well-being and provides a valuable example of lasting relationships for your children.

PRAYER

Dear Lord,

Guide me to nurture my friendships, strengthening these bonds as a source of joy, support, and growth in the journey of fatherhood.

Amen.

CHATTING WITH THE BIG GUY UPSTAIRS

6

"Trust in the Lord with all your heart and lean not on your own understanding."

– Proverbs 3:5

Have you ever felt uncertain about how to guide your children in this ever-changing, complex world? The key lies in deepening your connection with God, our ultimate role model. Strengthening your spiritual relationship is not just about prayer in times of need; it's about continuous dialogue and seeking wisdom in every aspect of parenting.

Consider incorporating daily moments of prayer and reflection into your routine. These moments don't have to be lengthy or formal. Even a few minutes of silent contemplation or a brief prayer for guidance while driving to work can make a significant difference. This constant conversation with God keeps your heart and mind open to His guidance, helping you make decisions that align with His teachings and embody the love and patience He shows us.

Remember, the goal is not to be a perfect parent but to be a present and God-centered one. Your efforts to connect with God and seek His guidance will not only benefit you but will also be a powerful example for your children.

DAD'S DUTY

Find a quiet moment to reflect on a specific parenting challenge you're facing. Bring this challenge to God in prayer, asking for His wisdom and guidance. Consider journaling any insights or thoughts that come to you during this time.

_____

_____

_____

_____

_____

_____

_____

_____

PRAYER

Dear Lord,

Guide me in my journey as a father. Let me lean on You for wisdom and strength, shaping my parenting in Your love and grace.

Amen.

FAITH IN THE FOG

"For we walk by faith, not by sight."
— 2 Corinthians 5:7

Have you ever found yourself in a situation where the path ahead as a father seems shrouded in uncertainty? You're not alone. Life can sometimes feel like stumbling through a dense fog, where the next steps are unclear, and the pressure to make the right choices can be overwhelming.

A father named Joseph faced unexpected challenges and found himself deep in the fog. His son was diagnosed with a learning disability. Joseph felt lost, unsure how to support his child or what the future might hold for them. Amidst this uncertainty, Joseph turned to his faith. He prayed not just for solutions but for the wisdom to guide his son through this challenge. Gradually, clarity emerged, not in the form of a miraculous solution, but in a deeper understanding and patience in his parenting.

Joseph's journey teaches us that in times of uncertainty, our faith is our compass. Trusting in God doesn't always provide immediate answers, but it gives us the strength to face challenges and the wisdom to find our way through them one step at a time. It teaches us to trust in a plan greater than our own, and to find peace in not having all the answers.

DAD'S DUTY

What area's in your life do you feel uncertain or lost? Spend time in prayer, asking not just for answers, but for the faith to trust in God's guidance, even when the path isn't clear. How can having this trust transform your approach to the challenge?

_____

_____

_____

_____

_____

_____

_____

_____

_____

PRAYER

Dear God,

In times of uncertainty, help me to walk by faith, trusting in Your guidance and finding strength in the unseen path You lay before me.

Amen.

NO 'I' IN PARENT

"Two are better than one, because they have a good return for their labor."

– Ecclesiastes 4:9

The truth is, fatherhood isn't a journey to be walked alone but a shared adventure with your partner. The strength of your family unit hinges not just on how you parent, but also on how you support and uplift your significant other. The essence of successful parenting lies in teamwork, mutual support, and shared visions with your significant other.

To be the best partner in this journey, the key is communication – not just the daily updates but deep, meaningful conversations about values, discipline, and the dreams you have for your children. It's about finding balance, understanding each other's parenting styles, and complementing rather than competing. Listen to your partner's needs and concerns with empathy and understanding. Acknowledge the efforts and sacrifices they make, often unseen and unspoken. Share household and parenting responsibilities equitably, understanding that teamwork in these areas strengthens your relationship and sets a positive example for your children. Just as a ship needs two well-coordinated hands on the wheel, your family thrives when both parents work in harmony.

Moreover, ensure that your partner feels valued not just as a co-parent but as an individual. Encourage their personal interests and aspirations. Make time for each other, away from the roles of parents, to nurture your relationship. This might mean planning regular date nights or simply spending quality time together after the kids are in bed.

DAD'S DUTY

Reflect on your relationship with your significant other beyond parenting. Identify one action you can take today to strengthen your partnership, whether it's helping with a task without being asked, planning a special moment together, or simply expressing your appreciation for them.

_____

_____

_____

_____

PRAYER

Dear Lord,

Guide me to be a supportive and loving partner, sharing the joys and burdens equally, strengthening our bond for the betterment of our family.

Amen.

"LETTING THEM FALL TO FLY": WATCHING THEM LEARN FROM LIFE'S LITTLE STUMBLES

"And we know that in all things God works for the good of those who love him, who have been called according to his purpose."

– ROMANS 8:28

Have you ever felt the urge to shield your child from every potential hurt or failure? It's a natural instinct, but part of our children's growth involves learning from their own experiences, including the missteps. Think about a time when you watched your child struggle, perhaps in learning a new skill or facing a challenge. The instinct to jump in and solve it for them is strong, but there's profound growth in struggle.

Consider the example of teaching a child to ride a bike. Those first wobbly attempts often lead to falls. As fathers, our role is not to prevent every fall, but to be there to encourage, guide, and comfort after each tumble. It's in getting back up that our children learn resilience, determination, and the joy of achievement.

This principle applies to all aspects of their lives. Whether it's navigating friendships, dealing with academic challenges, or making moral choices, our children learn and grow from each experience. Our job is to guide, support, and provide a safe environment for this growth, trusting that these experiences are shaping them into strong, capable individuals.

DAD'S DUTY

Reflect on a recent situation where you had to let your child face a challenge on their own. How did you feel? How did they handle it? Today, find an opportunity to encourage your child to take on a task or challenge independently, offering your support and guidance, but allowing them the space to grow and learn from the experience.

_____

_____

_____

_____

_____

PRAYER

Dear God,

Give me the wisdom to guide my children through life's challenges, teaching them resilience and strength, and trusting in Your plan for their growth.

Amen.

> **THE GREATEST MARK OF A FATHER IS HOW HE TREATS HIS CHILDREN WHEN NO ONE IS LOOKING.**
>
> – Dan Pearce

LESSONS, NOT LECTURES

10

"Fathers, do not exasperate your children; instead, bring them up in the training and instruction of the Lord."

– EPHESIANS 6:4

Have you ever found yourself at a crossroads of disciplining your child, wondering if there's a better way than stern lectures or harsh punishments? The truth is, effective discipline is less about punishment and more about teaching. It's about guiding our children to understand right from wrong and helping them learn from their mistakes.

Let's consider the approach of Michael, a father who believed in 'lessons, not lectures'. When his son broke a neighbor's window while playing, instead of reacting with immediate punishment, Michael used the situation as a teaching moment. He calmly discussed with his son why his actions were wrong and involved him in the process of apologizing and making amends. This approach not only taught his son responsibility but also empathy and problem-solving.

The key to Michael's approach was consistency. He was gentle yet firm, and his son knew what to expect. Being consistent in discipline, coupled with redirection and explanation, lays a solid foundation for understanding and internalizing right behaviors. It ensures that discipline is a learning process, not just a punishment for your child.

DAD'S DUTY

Think about a recent situation where you had to discipline your child. Reflect on how you handled it and consider if there was an opportunity for teaching rather than just punishment. Next time a disciplinary situation arises, take a moment to calmly explain the reasoning behind any consequences and involve your child in understanding and rectifying their mistake.

_____

_____

_____

_____

_____

_____

_____

PRAYER

Dear God,

Grant me the wisdom to guide my children with understanding and consistency, teaching them Your ways with love and patience rather than severity.

Amen.

THE UNFINISHED DAD   11

"But grow in the grace and knowledge of our Lord and Savior Jesus Christ."

– 2 Peter 3:18

Do you ever feel like you haven't quite figured out this whole 'dad' thing? You're not alone. Many fathers often think they need to have all the answers, but the truth is, fatherhood is a journey of continual growth and learning. Just like our walk with Christ, we are always evolving, always growing.

Think of fatherhood as a craft. Just as a skilled artisan never stops honing his craft, so too must you continually refine your skills as a father. It's about practice, patience, and learning from each experience, whether it's a moment of joy, a challenge, or even a mistake. Remember, each day is an opportunity to learn something new about yourself, your children, and how you can be a better dad.

Your journey as a father is unique and ongoing. Remember, your growth as a father is not measured by perfection but by the willingness to learn and adapt. Each stage of your child's life will bring new challenges and opportunities for growth. Be open to these experiences, embrace them, and use them to mold yourself into the father you aspire to be.

DAD'S DUTY

Spend some time reflecting on your own experiences as a child with your parents. Identify traits or actions of your parents that you admired and those you would do differently. Use these reflections to guide your actions and decisions as a dad.

_____

_____

_____

_____

_____

_____

_____

_____

PRAYER

Dear God,

Help me to embrace my journey as a father, always learning and growing in Your grace, and molding me into the dad You intend me to be.

Amen.

THE ART OF THE APOLOGY

12

"Therefore confess your sins to each other and pray for each other so that you may be healed. The prayer of a righteous person is powerful and effective."

– JAMES 5:16

Have you ever found it hard to swallow your pride and admit to your child that you were wrong? As fathers, we often feel the pressure to be infallible role models. But part of being a good father is showing our children that it's okay to be imperfect and that there's strength in admitting mistakes.

Take, for instance, the story of Tom, a dad who lost his temper over a minor mishap caused by his young son. After the moment passed, Tom realized that his reaction was harsher than the situation warranted. This realization wasn't easy for him, but he saw it as an essential teaching moment.

Tom sat down with his son, apologized for overreacting, and explained why he was wrong. In doing so, he taught his son a valuable lesson about humility and the importance of admitting mistakes. His son learned that everyone, even dads, can make errors in judgment, and that owning up to these mistakes is a sign of character and strength.

This act of vulnerability teaches your child that mistakes are part of being human and that owning up to them is a mark of character. It also helps to build trust and respect in your relationship, showing your child that you respect them enough to admit when you're wrong.

DAD'S DUTY

Reflect on a recent situation where you might have made a mistake in your parenting. Take the time today to talk to your child about it. Apologize sincerely, explaining why you were wrong and what you've learned. This conversation can be a stepping stone in building a deeper, more trusting relationship with your child.

_____

_____

_____

_____

PRAYER

Dear God,

Guide me to admit my faults to my children, teaching them through my example the value of humility, honesty, and the strength found in apology.

Amen.

TECH, TRENDS, AND TRADITIONS   13

"Do not conform to the pattern of this world, but be transformed by the renewing of your mind."
– ROMANS 12:2

In this era of rapid technological advancement, I think it's safe to say we've all found it challenging, at times, to balance the digital world with the real one. Navigating this digital landscape requires wisdom and discernment, especially when it comes to guiding our children through it.

The key is to find a balance. Embrace technology as a tool for learning and connection, but set boundaries to ensure it doesn't overshadow valuable family time, outdoor play, and face-to-face interactions. Encourage your children to appropriately explore and understand technology, but also to appreciate the richness of real-life experiences.

One practical way is to designate tech-free times in your household, such as during family meals or before bedtime. Use these moments to engage in traditional activities like reading together, playing board games, or simply talking about each other's day. These practices help inculcate values like family bonding, effective communication, and appreciation for the simpler things in life.

Remember, as a father, you are the navigator of this digital jungle. Your guidance can help your children use technology wisely while keeping them grounded in the real world and its enduring values.

DAD'S DUTY

Reflect on your family's current use of technology. Identify one area where you can create more balance, perhaps by introducing a tech-free family night or encouraging outdoor activities over the weekend. Implement this change and observe the impact it has on your family's interactions and overall well-being.

_____

_____

_____

_____

PRAYER

Dear God,

Help me to wisely guide my family in balancing technology with our cherished values, ensuring that our hearts and minds remain focused on what truly matters.

Amen.

DAD'S TIME-OUT

14

"Come to me, all you who are weary and burdened, and I will give you rest."

– Matthew 11:28

Have you ever felt overwhelmed by the relentless demands of fatherhood, forgetting when you last took a moment for yourself? It's a common experience for dads to put their own needs on the back burner. But remember, taking time for yourself isn't selfish – it's necessary.

David, a dedicated father and husband, always put his family's needs first. Over time, David began to feel burnt out, his joy and patience wearing thin. It wasn't until a close friend noticed and pointed out his exhaustion that David realized he hadn't taken any time for himself in months. This wake-up call led David to start scheduling regular "Dad's Time-Outs" – periods where he engaged in activities that rejuvenated him, be it a hobby, exercise, or simply quiet time for reflection and prayer.

These breaks not only restored David's energy and joy but also made him a more present and patient father and husband. By taking care of his own well-being, David found he had more to give to his family.

Taking time-out is not about escaping your responsibilities, but about recharging your spirit to fulfill them better. It's about finding balance and ensuring that you're the best version of yourself for your family. Recognize that by nurturing your well-being, you're not only helping yourself but also setting a positive example for self-care in your family.

DAD'S DUTY

Plan at least one activity this week that's just for you – something that recharges your batteries. It could be as simple as reading a book, going for a run, or spending quiet time in prayer.

_____

_____

_____

_____

_____

PRAYER

Dear Lord,

Grant me the wisdom to recognize the need for my own rest and rejuvenation, so I may serve You and my family with renewed spirit and joy.

Amen.

COUNTING BLESSINGS, NOT PROBLEMS

15

"Give thanks in all circumstances; for this is God's will for you in Christ Jesus."

– 1 Thessalonians 5:18

In the hustle of life, it's easy to focus on the challenges we face, while struggling to see any joy amidst the chaos. It's a common feeling, but there's profound strength in shifting our focus to the blessings, big and small, that fatherhood brings.

Every giggle, every heartfelt "I love you," every little hand reaching for yours, these are the treasures of fatherhood. It's in these instances that the beauty and wonder of being a dad are truly revealed. They remind us that amidst the trials and tribulations, there are countless reasons for gratitude and joy.

Learning to appreciate these small wonders is key to finding happiness in day-to-day life as a dad. These moments, though brief, are potent reminders of the love, curiosity, and joy that children bring into our lives.

DAD'S DUTY

Take a moment to identify and appreciate the small wonders in your day. It might be a giggle, a curious question, or a spontaneous moment of affection from your child. Make a mental note or write down these instances. Reflect on how they enrich your life and bring you joy, despite the challenges.

_____

_____

_____

_____

_____

_____

_____

_____

PRAYER

Dear God,

Help me to recognize and cherish the small blessings in my life as a father, finding joy and gratitude in every moment with my children.

Amen.

THE GRATEFUL DAD   16

"*Rejoice always, pray continually, give thanks in all circumstances; for this is God's will for you in Christ Jesus.*"

– 1 Thessalonians 5:16-18

What are you grateful for, today?

The art of gratitude is a vital life lesson to pass on to your kids. In a world often focused on what we lack, teaching our children the power of positivity and thankfulness can be transformative.

Being a 'Grateful Dad' means leading by example. It's about expressing thankfulness in everyday life, whether it's for a beautiful day, a kind gesture from a neighbor, or the joy your children bring into your life. This practice of gratitude doesn't ignore life's challenges but rather acknowledges and appreciates the good amidst them.

One practical way to cultivate this is by starting a family gratitude journal. Each evening, everyone in your family should write 3 things they were grateful for that day. This simple act not only fosters a positive outlook but also strengthens family bonds.

DAD'S DUTY

Actively look for moments or things to be thankful for and share them with your children. Initiate a conversation at dinner where each family member shares something they're grateful for.

_____

_____

_____

_____

_____

_____

_____

_____

PRAYER

Dear God,

Help me to be a model of gratitude for my children, teaching them to see Your blessings in every aspect of our lives with a thankful heart.

Amen.

JUGGLING THE DAILY GRIND & DAD DUTIES

17

"Whatever you do, work at it with all your heart, as working for the Lord, not for human masters."
– COLOSSIANS 3:23

Have you ever felt torn between the demands of your job and the precious family time? You're not alone. This balancing act is a common challenge for dads striving to provide for their family while also being an active part of their lives.

Take Alex's experience, instance. He worked long hours to ensure his family's financial stability, but then often found himself missing his son's soccer games and his daughter's school plays. Alex realized that while his hard work was necessary, he was missing out on irreplaceable moments. Alex began to make small but significant changes. He made a conscious decision to reevaluate his priorities and manage his time more effectively. By discussing his situation with his employer, he was able to adjust his schedule to attend important family events. This shift allowed him to be physically present for those milestones that matter both to him and his family.

Finding the right balance is about making deliberate choices. It involves assessing your priorities, effectively managing your time, and, at times, making difficult decisions for the greater good of your family. It's about recognizing that your presence in those little yet significant moments sends a powerful message to your children about what truly matters.

DAD'S DUTY

Reflect on your own work-life balance. How present are you in your family's lives? How could you make a small change to spend more time with your family?.

_____

_____

_____

_____

_____

_____

_____

PRAYER

Dear God,

Guide me in balancing my responsibilities, helping me to provide for my family while being present for the precious moments of our life together.

Amen.

RECHARGING DAD'S BATTERIES

18

"But they who wait for the Lord shall renew their strength; they shall mount up with wings like eagles; they shall run and not be weary; they shall walk and not faint."

– Isaiah 40:31

When was the last time you engaged in one of your favorite hobbies or interests? Do you ever feel as if your own passions are overshadowed by your parenting responsibilities?

Balancing fatherhood with personal passions is not only possible, but essential! Engaging in things you truly love recharges your batteries, giving you the energy and joy that you bring back into your role as a dad.

Think of it this way: When you're on an airplane, you're instructed to put on your oxygen mask before helping others. The same principle applies to parenting. Taking time for your hobbies is like giving yourself oxygen. It rejuvenates your spirit, sharpens your mind, and brings a sense of fulfillment that permeates all areas of your life, including your interactions with your children.

Your hobbies can also serve as a valuable lesson for your children. They learn to see you as an individual with interests and passions, which teaches them the importance of personal growth and finding balance in life. You never know, you might inspire them to one day take up your hobby themselves!

DAD'S DUTY

Reflect on your current hobbies or interests that you might have set aside. Take a step to reintegrate one of these activities into your life. It can be as simple as reading a book, playing a musical instrument, or working on a personal project. Notice how this recharges you and impacts your interactions with your family.

_____

_____

_____

_____

_____

_____

_____

PRAYER

Dear God,

Help me to find balance in nurturing my own passions and in my responsibilities as a father, knowing that both contribute to the wholeness of my family.

Amen.

> **THE GREATEST GIFT I EVER HAD CAME FROM GOD; I CALL HIM DAD!**
>
> – Unknown

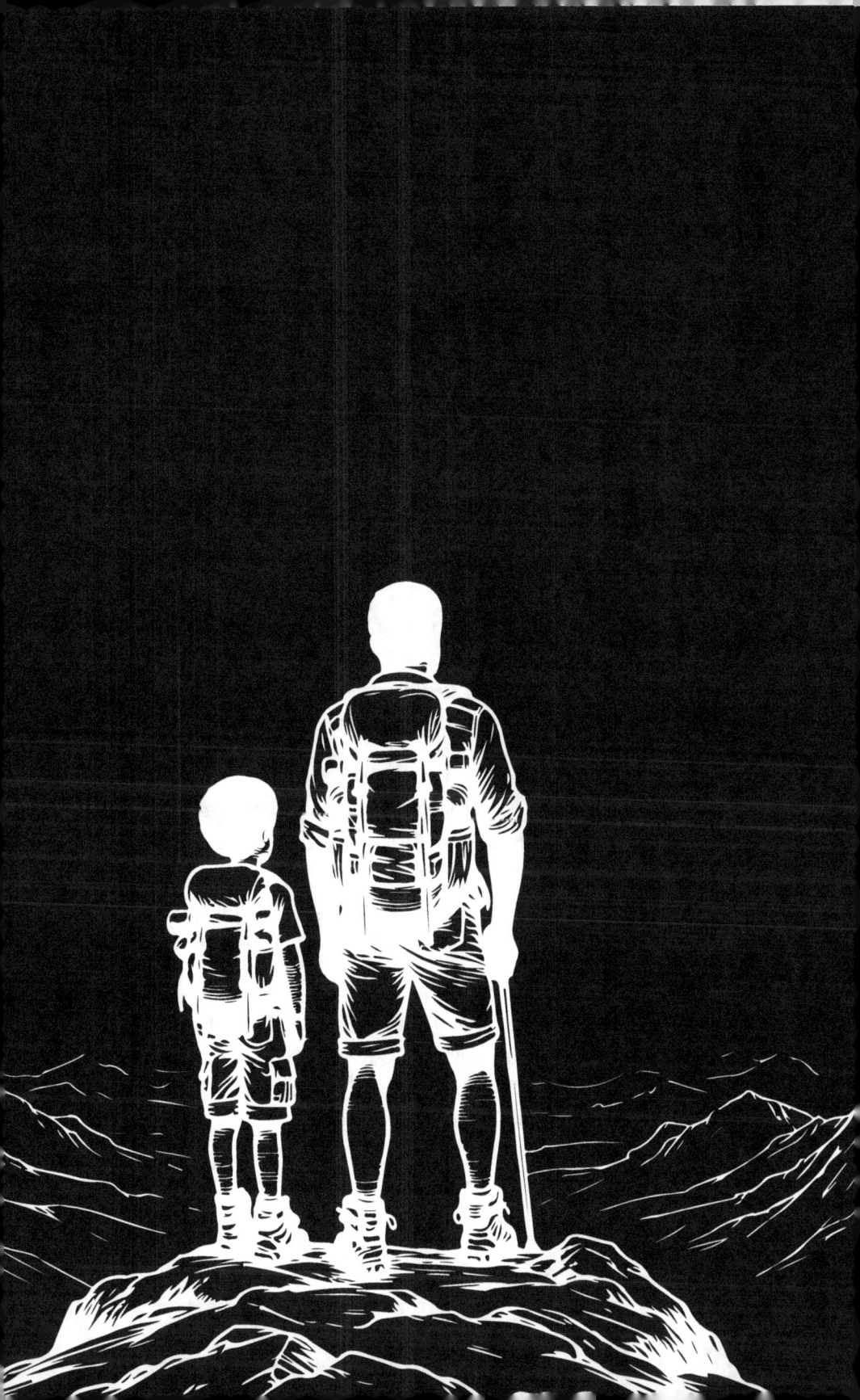

THE WORLD THROUGH THEIR EYES

19

"Train up a child in the way he should go; even when he is old he will not depart from it."
– PROVERBS 22:6

Have you ever paused to see the world from your child's perspective? Experiencing life through their eyes can open up a world of wonder and learning, not just for them, but for you as well. Exploring new places and learning new lessons together is an invaluable part of your journey as a father.

Imagine walking through a park with your child. To you, it may be a familiar path, but to them, it's a new adventure filled with wonders at every turn. Every leaf, bug, and puddle presents an opportunity for discovery and learning. When you embrace these moments, you're not only teaching your child about the world but also rekindling your own sense of curiosity and joy.

These shared experiences are the building blocks of lifelong learning and bonding. They remind us that fatherhood is not just about guiding our children, but also about growing with them, seeing the world anew through their eyes, and rediscovering the marvels of everyday life.

DAD'S DUTY

Plan an activity where you can explore and learn something new with your child. It could be a nature walk, a visit to a museum, or even trying out a new hobby together. Pay attention to what captures their interest and engage with them in that discovery process.

_____

_____

_____

_____

_____

_____

_____

_____

PRAYER

Dear Lord,

Help me to see the world through my child's eyes, embracing each moment of discovery and learning as a precious gift in our shared journey.

Amen.

MORE THAN JUST THE FUN DAD

20

"Bear one another's burdens, and so fulfill the law of Christ."

– Galatians 6:2

In a way, being a parent is like being a gardener. Just as a gardener nurtures plants with more than just sunlight—providing water, nutrients, and care—being a dad is more than being the source of fun. It's about being there emotionally for your children, providing support, understanding, and love in all seasons of their lives.

Take Jacob, one of the most fun-loving dads I've ever known. One evening, he noticed his daughter, Emma, seemed quieter than usual. Sensing something was amiss, Jacob gently asked her about her day. She opened up about feeling left out at school and being scared to go back.

In that moment, Jacob understood his role was more than just bringing smiles; it was also about providing a safe space for Emma to express her fears and sadness. He listened attentively, offering comforting words and reassurance. He shared his own childhood stories of overcoming fears, helping Emma feel understood and less alone. This experience deepened their bond, showing Emma that her dad was there for her emotionally, not just for fun times.

Your family needs you to be present in the quiet, more challenging moments —when they're struggling with a problem, facing a fear, or feeling sad. These are the times when your comfort, guidance, and listening ear are as crucial as your ability to bring joy.

DAD'S DUTY

Take time to truly listen to your child. Whether they're facing a fear, a challenge, or just need to talk, be there to listen, understand, and support them. Your emotional presence can make all the difference.

_____

_____

_____

_____

_____

PRAYER

Dear Lord,

Empower me to be a source of strength and comfort to my children, standing by them in both their joys and their struggles.

Amen.

TEAMWORK MAKES THE DREAM WORK

21

"Two are better than one because they have a good reward for their toil."

– Ecclesiastes 4:9

Being a super dad also means being a stellar partner. The strength and health of your relationship with your significant other greatly impact the overall well-being of your family.

Balancing these roles is about more than dividing chores or scheduling date nights. It's about cultivating a partnership grounded in mutual respect, understanding, and support. This means actively listening to your partner, appreciating their contributions to the family, and being attentive to their emotional needs. It also involves showing empathy, sharing responsibilities, and working together to overcome the challenges of parenting - as a team!

Every gesture of support and understanding towards your partner not only strengthens your relationship but also sets a powerful example for your children. Children thrive in a nurturing and loving environment. They will learn how to love, respect, and cooperate with their own future partners, just from the way you treat your significant other. Teach them well, because these lessons will guide them throughout their lives.

Your family needs you to be present in the quiet, more challenging moments —when they're struggling with a problem, facing a fear, or feeling sad. These are the times when your comfort, guidance, and listening ear are as crucial as your ability to bring joy.

DAD'S DUTY

Reflect on your partnership within your family dynamic. Find a way to show appreciation to your partner, whether it's helping with a task, planning a special moment, or simply expressing gratitude for their presence in your life.

_____

_____

_____

_____

_____

PRAYER

Dear God,

Guide me to be a supportive partner and a loving father, strengthening our family with the harmony of teamwork, love, and mutual respect.

Amen.

THE ART OF THE GENTLE NO

22

"Let your 'Yes' be yes, and your 'No,' no, or you will be condemned."

— James 5:12

How often do you find yourself in a position where you need to set limits with your children? Probably quite a lot, right? It's a familiar scenario: your child asks for something inappropriate or at an inopportune time, and you're faced with the delicate task of saying 'no' in a way that is both loving and firm.

My friend Anthony often finds himself at a crossroads with his daughter's growing demands. How he handles her requests is a delicate balancing act. Lily, energetic and curious, frequently asks for things like extra screen time or sweets before dinner. Anthony, understanding the importance of healthy boundaries, knew he had to say 'no' but wanted to do it in a way that Lily would understand and accept. He made it a practice to explain his reasons gently and provide alternative options. For instance, instead of more screen time, he would suggest a board game they could play together, turning a moment of refusal into an opportunity for connection.

Anthony's approach is one we can all take note of as it shows his daughter that while boundaries were necessary, they were set with her best interests at heart. His gentle but firm 'no' helped Lily learn about limits and respect, fostering her ability to make better choices moving forward.

DAD'S DUTY

Reflect on how you set boundaries with your children. When a situation arises where you need to set a limit - practice the art of the gentle 'no.' Do it with firmness but also with love, offering an explanation and an alternative if possible.

_____

_____

_____

_____

_____

_____

_____

PRAYER

Dear God,

Guide me in setting boundaries with kindness and firmness, helping me to nurture my child's growth with love, understanding, and respect.

Amen.

FIT DAD, FUN DAD

"Do you not know that your bodies are temples of the Holy Spirit, who is in you, whom you have received from God? You are not your own."
– 1 Corinthians 6:19

Have you truly pondered how your physical well-being directly influences your role as an engaged and active parent? It's a profound thought. Staying physically fit is more than a personal health goal; it's a critical component of being there for your children, not just in spirit but in every sprint, every throw, every adventure.

Physical fitness for fathers extends well beyond the realms of a gym. It's in those everyday moments – playing catch, exploring nature trails, teaching your child to ride a bike – where its true value shines. It's about having the stamina to be part of those precious, fleeting moments of childhood, creating memories that will last a lifetime.

But more importantly, ask yourself, how does your commitment to physical health model a lifestyle for your children? In demonstrating the importance of fitness, you are setting a precedent for them, teaching them, without words, the value of taking care of the body God has given us.

helped Lily learn about limits and respect, fostering her ability to make better choices moving forward.

DAD'S DUTY

Find a way to incorporate physical activity into your time with your children. Whether it's a game of catch, a bike ride, or a playful race in the park, let this shared experience be a fun, bonding moment and a lesson in valuing health and wellness.

_____

_____

_____

_____

_____

_____

_____

_____

PRAYER

Dear Lord,

Empower me to be a beacon of health and activity for my children, showing them through my actions the importance of caring for the body You've given us.

Amen.

PENNY-WISE PARENTING

24

"The plans of the diligent lead to profit as surely as haste leads to poverty."

– Proverbs 21:5

Do you ever feel the weight of your family's financial future on your shoulders? Managing finances can be a daunting task, but it's also an opportunity to teach valuable life lessons and secure your family's future. It's about being 'penny-wise' – making smart, well-planned financial decisions and teaching your children the value of money and hard work.

Balancing the budget, saving for the future, and still fulfilling the needs and some wants of your family requires wisdom and patience. It's important to involve your family in financial discussions appropriate for their age. This can range from explaining why saving is important, to involving older children in budgeting for a family outing. These practices not only help in managing finances better but also prepare your children for their financial future.

Remember, managing finances is not just about making ends meet; it's about making wise choices that can turn dreams into reality, all while maintaining a sense of calm and trust in God's provision.

DAD'S DUTY

Think of one area of your family's finances that you can improve. It might be creating a more detailed budget, starting a savings plan for your child's education, or simply cutting back on unnecessary expenses. How can you involve your family in this?

_____
_____
_____
_____
_____
_____
_____

PRAYER

Dear Lord,

Guide me to manage my family's finances with wisdom and diligence, providing for their needs, securing our future, and teaching them the value of prudent living.

Amen.

MENTAL FITNESS FOR FATHERS 25

"For God has not given us a spirit of fear, but of power and of love and of a sound mind."
— 2 Timothy 1:7

Just as a captain must be alert and clear-headed to steer his ship through stormy seas, a dad needs mental fitness to traverse the complexities of family life. Your mental state sets the tone for your household; it's the rudder that steers your family's emotional and psychological well-being.

Picture your mind as a garden. Neglect it, and weeds of stress, anxiety, and negativity can overrun it. Tend to it, and it can flourish, positively influencing both you and your family. Developing your mental fitness involves regular practices like prayer, meditation, and self-reflection. It also means seeking support when needed, embracing community, and taking time for activities that rejuvenate your spirit.

Your mental health is a cornerstone of your family's health. By maintaining it, you not only ensure your well-being but also foster a nurturing environment for your family.

DAD'S DUTY

Take some time for an activity that benefits your mental health. It could be a quiet moment of prayer, a walk, reading, or pursuing a hobby. Acknowledge this practice as not just self-care, but as an essential part of being the best dad you can be.

_____

_____

_____

_____

_____

_____

_____

_____

PRAYER

Dear God,

Strengthen my mind and spirit, that I may be a source of stability and love for my family, reflecting Your peace and wisdom in all I do.

Amen.

TOUGH TALKS: LIFE, LOSS, AND LOVE

26

"Even though I walk through the darkest valley, I will fear no evil, for you are with me; your rod and your staff, they comfort me."

– PSALM 23:4

Have you ever faced the daunting task of explaining the finality of death to your child? This is where fatherhood extends into being a guide through life's most profound mysteries. Meet Noah, a father who recently faced this challenge when the family dog, whom they had loved for years, passed away. His young daughter, Sophia, was filled with questions and sorrow.

Noah realized this was more than just a conversation about loss; it was a pivotal moment to teach about the cycle of life, love, and the reality of loss. He sat down with Sophia, his heart heavy but his resolve clear. He spoke honestly and gently, using the metaphor of seasons changing to explain death as a natural part of life. He shared his belief in an afterlife, offering comfort and hope.

This talk, though difficult, brought Noah and Sophia closer. It showed her that her dad was there for her in the toughest times, ready to face life's hard truths together. Noah's approach exemplified the strength and sensitivity needed in navigating these tough talks.

DAD'S DUTY

Reflect on how you would handle a conversation about loss and love with your child. Consider the values and beliefs you'd want to convey. Perhaps write down a few key points or metaphors you could use to help explain these complex topics in an age-appropriate way.

_____

_____

_____

_____

_____

_____

_____

_____

_____

PRAYER

Dear Lord,

Grant me the wisdom and words to guide my child through life's toughest lessons, offering comfort, understanding, and strength in times of loss and change.

Amen.

MAKE A DIFFERENCE WITH YOUR REVIEW

"In the quiet moments of reflection, we find our greatest strength. Devotion isn't just about personal growth; it's about extending that growth outward, selflessly aiding others on their own spiritual journeys."

- ANONYMOUS

Hey there, Super Dad!

If we've got a shot at spreading joy and wisdom during our time together, let's give it our all. I have a small yet mighty favor to ask...

Would you be willing to help a fellow dad on his journey, even if you never meet him?

A dad who is struggling to manage the delicate balance of parenting. He's got to protect his crown as the reigning champion of the grill, continue being the reliable wheel behind 'Dad's Taxi', and nurture his family in precious moments as Papa Bear. All the while, he's striving to find a moment of peace for himself amidst the bustling duties of fatherhood. Just like you, he's riding the highs and lows of fatherhood.

Our mission with *Men's Devotional For Dads* is to reach dads everywhere - those in the trenches of parenthood, looking for a beacon of light and a dash of humor. We want to make these devotions as accessible as dad jokes at a family BBQ.

Here's where you come into play. Reviews are the lifeblood of any book, guiding others to make informed choices. So, on behalf of a dad out there who could use a little guidance...

Please consider leaving a review for our book.

It's a simple act of kindness - quick, cost-free, but immensely powerful. Your words could be the very thing another dad needs to hear. Your review might inspire...

...a new dad navigating the world of discipline and guidance for the first time.
...a seasoned dad looking for fresh parenting perspectives.
...a dad seeking to balance work, family, and personal growth.
...or a dad yearning for community and fellowship.

To leave your mark and spread the dad love, just scan this QR code:

[https://www.amazon.com/review/review-your-purchases/?asin=BOOKASIN]

Thanks a million! Your review not only uplifts another dad but also fuels our mission to support fathers in every walk of life.

With your help, we're not just sharing a book; we're building a movement. Now, let's get back to tackling dad life with gusto and grace.

Cheers,
Your biggest fan, Biblical Teachings

P.S. - Fun fact: Sharing is caring! If you've found value in this devotional and know another dad who'd benefit from it, pass this book along. Let's keep the wisdom flowing!

GUIDE, DON'T GOAD   27

"Listen, my son, to your father's instruction and do not forsake your mother's teaching. They are a garland to grace your head and a chain to adorn your neck."

— Proverbs 1:8-9

How often have you felt the need to discipline, and how do you strike the balance between correction and guidance? It's crucial to remember that effective discipline is not merely about correcting wrong behavior; it's fundamentally about teaching and leading our children on the path of righteousness with understanding and compassion.

Let's delve deeper into a scenario where your child has made a mistake. Before jumping to punishment, take a step back and engage in a dialogue with your child. Try to understand their thought process and feelings that led to their actions. This kind of empathetic listening allows your child to feel heard and valued, even in moments of discipline.

Once their perspective is clear, gently guide them to see why their behavior was inappropriate. Discuss the possible consequences of their actions, not only for themselves but for others involved. This method helps them develop empathy and a sense of responsibility. Then, collaboratively explore how they might handle a similar situation differently in the future. This process teaches them critical thinking and problem-solving skills, vital for their personal growth.

Moreover, it's important to model the behaviors you wish to instill in your children. They learn much from observing how you handle your mistakes. Admitting your own errors and apologizing when necessary shows them that making mistakes is a natural part of life and that owning them is a sign of strength and character.

DAD'S DUTY

Reflect on how you handle disciplinary situations. Today, commit to practicing empathetic listening and guiding conversations that lead to learning and growth, rather than mere correction. Remember, your approach to discipline is a powerful tool in shaping your child's character and worldview.

PRAYER

Dear God,

Guide me in my role as a father to discipline with love, understanding, and patience, teaching my children Your ways and modeling Christ-like grace and wisdom.

Amen.

TRAINING WHEELS TO WINGS

28

"I will instruct you and teach you in the way you should go; I will counsel you with my loving eye on you."

– Psalm 32:8

Have you ever thought about the transition from holding your child's hand to watching them walk their path independently? This journey from 'training wheels to wings' is one of the most vital tasks you will undertake as a parent. It involves guiding your child from a place of dependency to becoming a self-reliant, responsible adult.

Imagine your child's life as a bicycle ride. Initially, you're their training wheels, providing balance and security as they learn to pedal. As they grow, your role shifts to running alongside them, ready to catch them if they fall. Eventually, the day comes to let go, trusting in their ability to ride alone. This transition isn't easy – it requires patience, trust, and the courage to step back.

Your guidance during these stages is crucial. It's about teaching them the value of hard work, the importance of responsibility, and the resilience to overcome obstacles. This preparation is what gives them the confidence to soar on their own.

DAD'S DUTY

Reflect on how you are currently guiding your child towards independence. Today, identify one area where you can encourage more self-reliance, whether it's a simple household chore or a decision they can make on their own. Trust in their ability to handle this new responsibility.

_____
_____
_____
_____
_____
_____
_____
_____

PRAYER

Dear God,

Guide me in nurturing my child's growth from dependence to independence, equipping them with strength, wisdom, and courage to navigate life's journey with faith and confidence.

Amen.

STAND UP, STAND OUT 29

"Do not be misled: 'Bad company corrupts good character.'"

– 1 Corinthians 15:33

Have you ever watched your child grapple with the desire to fit in, while also wanting to stand true to their values? Handling peer pressure is a significant challenge for children and teens. Let's dive into the story of Jacob, a father who noticed his teenage son, Reece, wrestling with these pressures.

Over a few months Jacob observed negative changes in Reece's behavior, and who he was hanging around with. One day, he decided to address it. Instead of lecturing, Jacob chose a walk-and-talk approach. During their walk, he shared his own experiences with peer pressure, emphasizing the importance of staying true to one's values. This open and honest communication allowed Reece to express his fears and uncertainties regarding his new-found friends and the activities they wanted him to participate in.

Jacob's approach was not to dictate Reece's choices but to guide him in making decisions that aligned with his personal values and beliefs, not his friend's. This conversation opened the door for ongoing dialogue about these challenges. This feeling of safety and non-judgement allowed Reece to continue to open up with any issues that arose as he continued his journey into adulthood and beyond.

DAD'S DUTY

Reflect on how you can open a conversation about peer pressure with your child. Today, initiate a casual but meaningful talk, sharing your experiences and listening to theirs. Use this as a starting point for ongoing discussions about standing firm in their beliefs.

_____
_____
_____
_____
_____
_____
_____
_____
_____

PRAYER

Dear God,

Equip me with wisdom to guide my child through social challenges, teaching them to stand firm in their faith and values amidst the pressures of the world.

Amen.

THE CONFIDENCE COACH

"I can do all things through Christ who strengthens me."

– Philippians 4:13

As a dad, you have a significant impact on your child's self-confidence. Think of yourself as a 'Confidence Coach', not just in words, but through your actions and the environment you create for your family. It's not just about the encouragement you give; it's also about how you guide them to see and overcome challenges.

One effective approach is setting up small, achievable goals for your child. Acknowledge and celebrate each accomplishment, showing them that their efforts are valued. Share your own experiences of facing and overcoming challenges, emphasizing that perseverance and faith are key to success.

Equally important is creating a safe space for your child to take risks and make mistakes. Help them understand that failures are not setbacks but opportunities for growth and learning. This understanding helps them realize that their value does not hinge on being perfect but on the effort and the journey of learning.

These methods can help your child to understand their worth is not tied to perfection, and each failure is a stepping stone to success. Slowly, but steadily, your children will develop unwavering self-belief!

DAD'S DUTY

Reflect on your child's current challenges. Find a way today to help them set a small, achievable goal. Celebrate their effort and progress, not just the outcome, reinforcing their belief in their abilities and the strength they gain through Christ.

_____

_____

_____

_____

_____

_____

_____

_____

PRAYER

Dear God,

Guide me to nurture my child's confidence, celebrating their efforts and resilience, and teaching them to find strength and self-belief through their faith in You.

Amen.

DAD, THE PEACEKEEPER

"Blessed are the peacemakers, for they will be called children of God."
— Matthew 5:9

We've all found ourselves in the middle of a family disagreement before, struggling to reach the eye of the storm. As dads, we're often called to be the peacekeepers in our families. The ability to maintain composure during conflicts is a vital skill we must attain.

Imagine a scenario where your children are arguing loudly over a game. The noise escalates, and tension fills the room. It's in these moments that your role as a peacekeeper is crucial. Instead of adding to the chaos with frustration or anger, take a deep breath and approach the situation with a calm demeanor. Your composed presence can immediately diffuse the tension.

By calmly addressing each child, listening to their viewpoints, and guiding them towards a resolution, you not only resolve the immediate conflict but also teach them valuable lessons in communication and understanding. It's about showing them how to navigate disagreements with respect and empathy, a skill they'll carry into adulthood.

DAD'S DUTY

The next time a conflict arises in your family, take a moment to center yourself before responding. Approach the situation calmly, listen to all sides, and guide your family towards a peaceful resolution. Your approach to conflict can teach your children invaluable lessons about peace and understanding.

_____

_____

_____

_____

_____

_____

_____

PRAYER

Dear God,

Grant me the patience and wisdom to be a peacemaker in my family, guiding conflicts to calm and teaching my children the value of peace and understanding.

Amen.

LOVE LESSONS AT HOME

32

"Above all, love each other deeply, because love covers over a multitude of sins."

— 1 Peter 4:8

Have you ever considered how your relationship with your partner serves as the first classroom for your children's understanding of love and relationships? One couple knew this so decided to make a conscious effort to model a healthy relationship in their home.

Denzel and Sarah faced their fair share of challenges, but they committed to resolving conflicts with respect, communicating openly, and demonstrating affection and support for each other. They made it a point to show appreciation and to work as a team, even in small daily tasks.

Their children, Luke and Anna, grew up observing this dance of love and respect. They saw their parents navigate disagreements with understanding and forgiveness. They witnessed moments of kindness, laughter, and teamwork. This environment shaped their perception of what a healthy relationship should look like.

As Luke and Anna entered their own adult relationships, the lessons from home became evident. They approached relationships with the same respect, communication, and love they had witnessed growing up. Denzel and Sarah's example had laid a strong foundation for their children, guiding them to form healthy, loving relationships of their own.

DAD'S DUTY

Engage your family in a relationship workshop. Discuss and note down key healthy relationship behaviors on notecards. Each week, pick a behavior to focus on, practicing and acknowledging it within the family. Conclude with a weekly reflection to discuss the impact and growth in your family dynamics.

_____

_____

_____

_____

_____

PRAYER

Dear God,

Help me exemplify a loving, respectful relationship in my home, guiding my children by example to understand and cherish the true essence of love and partnership.

Amen.

THE VALUE OF A DOLLAR

33

"The wise store up choice food and olive oil, but fools gulp theirs down."
– Proverbs 21:20

Sooner or later, we all have to teach our children about money. Teaching your kids the value of a dollar is more than a lesson in finance; it's a lesson in responsibility, foresight, and stewardship.

In a world where instant gratification is the norm, how do you instill in your children the virtue of saving and the wisdom of prudent spending? It starts with simple, everyday actions. Introduce a piggy bank for younger children, encouraging them to save a portion of their allowance. For older kids, consider opening a savings account or involving them in planning and saving for a family goal, like a vacation or a big purchase.

These practices teach children that money is a resource to be managed wisely. It's about balancing between saving for the future (like college funds) and enjoying the present responsibly. By involving your children in financial decisions appropriate for their age, you're laying the foundation for financial wisdom and independence.

DAD'S DUTY

Set up a savings goal activity. Have your child pick an item they wish to buy. Calculate its cost and determine how much they need to save weekly. Track progress on a chart, celebrating milestones together. Teaches goal-setting and the value of saving!

_____

_____

_____

_____

_____

_____

_____

PRAYER

Dear God,

Help me teach my children the value of money, guiding them to use it wisely, save diligently, and give generously, reflecting responsible stewardship in Your eyes.

Amen.

THE LAND OF NOD   34

"In peace I will lie down and sleep, for you alone, Lord, make me dwell in safety."
– Psalm 4:8

Ahh, bedtime. The time we always hope to be a peaceful end to the day is usually anything but. Ring any bells?

Mastering the bedtime routine is crucial not only for ensuring your children sleep well but also for the numerous benefits that adequate sleep brings. A consistent, calming bedtime routine can greatly improve the quality of sleep for both you and your children. Good sleep has been shown to enhance mood, increase attention span, and boost overall health and well-being. It plays a vital role in physical health, aiding in the healing and repair of the heart and blood vessels, and supports growth and development in children.

For you, as a dad, ensuring a good night's rest for your children can also mean better sleep for yourself, leading to improved mental clarity, emotional well-being, and energy levels. This, in turn, enables you to be more present, patient, and effective in your parenting.

Remember, by establishing and maintaining a peaceful bedtime routine, you're not only helping your children to drift off into the Land of Nod more easily but also investing in their long-term health and happiness, as well as your own.

DAD'S DUTY

Create a consistent bedtime routine with your family. Include a calming activity like reading a book or discussing the day. Observe how this affects the ease of getting them to sleep and the quality of their rest, and how it affects you.

_____

_____

_____

_____

_____

_____

_____

_____

PRAYER

Dear Lord,

Bless our bedtime routine with peace and calm. Guide me in creating a restful end to the day for my children, fostering comfort and security.

Amen.

SELF-CARE ISN'T SELFISH

Have you ever felt too drained to engage fully with your family?

So too, did Franklin. He often put his needs last, leading to exhaustion and irritability. One day, his daughter asked why he never laughed anymore. This question was a wake-up call.

Realizing the importance of self-care, Franklin started setting aside time for his well-being. He began with regular exercise, which improved his physical health and energy levels. He also dedicated time each week to his hobby of woodworking, which brought him mental relaxation and a sense of accomplishment. Additionally, Franklin made sure to have quiet time for prayer and reflection, nourishing his spiritual health.

These acts of self-care had profound benefits. Franklin's mood improved, making him more patient and present with his family. His increased energy meant he could engage in more activities with his children, creating joyful and lasting memories. His commitment to self-care also taught his children the importance of prioritizing their own health and happiness.

Remember, self-care isn't selfish – it's essential.

DAD'S DUTY

Write a list of ways you can practice self-care. Pick one and get stuck in today! (Even if it's just for 5 minutes)

_____
_____
_____
_____
_____
_____
_____
_____
_____

PRAYER

Dear Lord,

Help me to understand the importance of self-care, and guide me to nurture my own well-being as a way of being my best for my family.

Amen.

> "A GOOD FATHER IS ONE OF THE MOST UNSUNG, UNPRAISED, UNNOTICED, AND YET ONE OF THE MOST VALUABLE ASSETS IN OUR SOCIETY.
>
> – Billy Graham

THE 'GOOD ENOUGH' DAD

36

"For we are God's handiwork, created in Christ Jesus to do good works, which God prepared in advance for us to do."
— Ephesians 2:10

In a world that strives for perfection, the truth is, being a 'good enough' dad – someone who acknowledges and celebrates his wins while learning from his shortcomings – is far more impactful and realistic. Fatherhood is a continuous path of learning and growth.

Every dad experiences moments of triumph – those heartwarming instances where everything just seems to click. It could be successfully teaching your child to ride a bike or having a meaningful conversation with them. These are the wins to be celebrated and cherished.

Then there are times that don't go as planned, which are just as valuable. These not-so-wins, like losing patience or missing an important event, aren't failures but opportunities for self-reflection and growth. They are moments to teach your children about humility, the importance of apologizing, and the reality that everyone, even dads, are continuously learning and improving.

DAD'S DUTY

Create a 'Win Jar' with your family. Each time you have a win or learn from a mistake, write it down and put it in the jar. Regularly review these notes as a family, celebrating and learning together.

_____

_____

_____

_____

_____

_____

_____

_____

PRAYER

Dear God,

Help me embrace both my successes and failures in fatherhood, learning and growing in Your grace, and showing my children the value of perseverance and humility.

Amen.

CHIEF CHEERLEADER & #1 FAN

37

"Encourage one another and build each other up, just as in fact you are doing."

– 1 Thessalonians 5:11

Whether it's in sports, arts, academics, or any other pursuit, your support and encouragement can be the driving force behind their confidence and passion.

This role goes beyond mere attendance at events or congratulatory words. It's about showing genuine interest in what they love, celebrating their efforts regardless of the outcome, and providing encouragement during both successes and setbacks. This consistent support tells your child that you value their interests and believe in their potential, which is a powerful motivator for them to pursue their passions and goals.

Your role as their #1 fan also includes guiding them to handle both triumph and disappointment gracefully, teaching them the value of perseverance, and instilling in them a healthy perspective on success and failure. Because of YOU, they'll have improved self-esteem and develop into well-rounded individuals during adulthood.

DAD'S DUTY

Get involved in an activity your kid loves. It doesn't matter what it is, even if you find it stupid - get involved and genuinely be curious. Find out what they love about it, and encourage them to keep on going.

_____

_____

_____

_____

_____

_____

_____

_____

PRAYER

Dear Lord,

Guide me to be a source of unwavering support and encouragement for my child, celebrating their passions and fostering their growth in love and confidence.

Amen.

BIRDS AND THE BEES 38

"By wisdom a house is built, and through understanding it is established; through knowledge its rooms are filled with rare and beautiful treasures."
– Proverbs 24:3-4

Have you wondered when the right time is to have 'the talk' about the birds and the bees? It's a topic that many dads approach with apprehension, yet it's crucial your kids learn about this. The key is not to wait for a single, grand moment, but to build a foundation of openness and trust over time.

The journey of discussing the birds and the bees with your child can be approached in stages, each tailored to their age and understanding. For example, with younger children, it might start with discussions about body safety and respect. As they grow, these conversations can evolve to include topics about changes during puberty, emphasizing the importance of respect and care in relationships.

Thomas initiated these talks with his son, Lucas, when he was young. Thomas began with simple conversations about respecting personal space and understanding body boundaries. As Lucas entered his pre-teen years, Thomas expanded these talks to include discussions about puberty, always in an age-appropriate and respectful manner. By the time Lucas was a teenager, Thomas had established a foundation of trust and openness, making conversations about relationships and responsibility natural and less daunting. This gradual approach allowed Lucas to absorb the information at his own pace and fostered a deeper understanding and respect for the topic.

DAD'S DUTY

Consider starting a journal with your child where you both can write down questions and thoughts about growing up, relationships, and related topics. Regularly review and discuss these entries together in a relaxed setting, and answer any questions they have.

_____

_____

_____

_____

_____

PRAYER

Dear God,

Guide me in providing wise and loving counsel to my child about life's delicate topics, fostering an environment of trust, respect, and understanding.

Amen.

THE FAMILY THAT PLAYS TOGETHER...

"Let each of us please his neighbor for his good, to build him up."

– Romans 15:2

Have you ever considered how sharing your hobbies and passions with your family can strengthen your bonds and create lasting memories? It's not just about spending time together; it's about inviting your children into your world of interests and, in doing so, connecting with them on a deeper level.

Imagine the joy and learning that comes from involving your children in activities you love. Whether it's gardening, woodworking, playing a musical instrument, or hiking, these experiences offer unique opportunities for bonding. They allow your children to see another side of you, beyond just being 'Dad.' These shared experiences become a platform for teaching, learning, and growing together.

This isn't about forcing your interests on them, but about opening a door to your world. It's an invitation for them to explore and, perhaps, develop their own passion for these activities. Even more, it's a way to teach values such as patience, perseverance, and the joy of learning.

DAD'S DUTY

Plan a family activity centered around one of your hobbies. Whether it's a cooking session, a bike ride, or a DIY project at home, involve your family in a fun and engaging way.

_____
_____
_____
_____
_____
_____
_____
_____
_____

PRAYER

Dear God,

Guide me in sharing my passions with my family, using these moments to strengthen our bonds, teach valuable lessons, and create joyous, lasting memories together.

Amen.

WALKING THE DAD WALK

"Set an example for the believers in speech, in conduct, in love, in faith and in purity."
— 1 Timothy 4:12

Do you realize the impact of your everyday actions on your children's understanding of what it means to be a good person? Let's reflect on the story of Mr. Johnson, a father who realized the power of his example in shaping his children's character.

One day, Mr. Johnson took his two sons, Jack and Sam, to a local food drive. As they worked together sorting and distributing food, he explained why helping those in need was important. This experience was more than just a lesson in charity; it was a practical demonstration of compassion and community service.

The boys saw their father engage respectfully with every person they met, showing kindness and understanding, without judgment based on who they were, or where they were in life. This left a lasting impression on them. As they grew, Jack and Sam began to emulate these qualities, often volunteering and showing empathy in their interactions with others. They had learned from their father that being a good person involved actions, not just words.

What kind of person do you want your children to grow up to be? Show them with your actions. It all starts with you.

DAD'S DUTY

Engage in an act of kindness or service with your children. Use this opportunity to demonstrate the values you wish to instill in them, such as compassion, respect, or generosity.

_____
_____
_____
_____
_____
_____
_____
_____
_____

PRAYER

Dear Lord,

Help me to walk the path of righteousness, setting an example for my children in my actions and deeds, guiding them to live lives of love and integrity.

Amen.

FUELING THEIR FIRE   41

"Whatever you do, work at it with all your heart, as working for the Lord, not for human masters."
– Colossians 3:23

How often do you recognize and nurture the unique passions and interests that burn within your children? Encouraging their aspirations is not just about providing resources or opportunities; it's about actively engaging with their dreams and showing genuine interest and support, without imposing our own desires or expectations.

Reflect on the story of Andrew, a father who noticed his daughter, Rachel's, growing interest in astronomy. Instead of steering her towards his own interests, Andrew embraced her passion. He spent evenings with Rachel stargazing, learning about constellations, and even organized a visit to a local observatory. This shared journey did more than just fuel Rachel's passion for astronomy; it strengthened their bond and boosted her self-confidence. Andrew's encouragement and openness to her unique interests showed Rachel that her passions were valuable and worth pursuing, which was instrumental in her continued passion and growth in the field.

Andrew's approach serves as a reminder that our children are individuals with their own talents and aspirations. Our role as fathers is to support and encourage these unique qualities, helping them to develop into the person they are meant to be, not necessarily who we imagined they would be.

DAD'S DUTY

Identify an interest or passion your child has. Plan an activity that supports and engages with this interest, whether it's a project, a visit to a relevant site, or a simple home-based activity. Show your child that their passions are worth exploring and celebrating.

_____

_____

_____

_____

_____

_____

_____

PRAYER

Dear God,

Guide me to nurture the unique gifts and passions in my child, encouraging them to pursue their dreams with confidence and joy, in Your guiding light.

Amen.

PERFECTLY IMPERFECT DAD

 *"But he said to me, 'My grace is sufficient for you, for my power is made perfect in weakness.' Therefore I will boast all the more gladly about my weaknesses, so that Christ's power may rest on me."*
— 2 Corinthians 12:9

Have you ever felt the pressure to match up to an ideal image of fatherhood, only to realize that perfection is an unattainable goal? Embracing your unique fathering style means acknowledging that you are 'perfectly imperfect'. Your individual strengths, quirks, and even weaknesses contribute to the special bond you share with your children.

Peter always felt a little different from other fathers. He wasn't athletic or handy with tools, but he had a passion for music and literature. Initially, Peter felt inadequate compared to other dads, but he soon realized that his unique interests were a gift to his children. He shared his love of books and music with them, leading to shared moments of discovery and joy. Peter's children learned to appreciate and embrace their own uniqueness.

Peter's story teaches us that being a father isn't about fitting a standard mold. It's about being authentic and sharing your true self with your children. Your individuality is what makes your relationship with your children special.

Remember - there isn't another you! Being different is cool and unique.

DAD'S DUTY

Reflect on what makes your fathering style unique. Today, share a part of your authentic self with your children, whether it's a hobby, a story, or a lesson from your life. Embrace and celebrate your individuality as a dad.

_____

_____

_____

_____

_____

_____

_____

PRAYER

Dear God,

Help me to embrace my unique qualities as a father, understanding that in my imperfections, Your grace shines, guiding me to connect authentically with my children.

Amen.

LISTENING EARS, SPEAKING HEARTS

43

"Everyone should be quick to listen, slow to speak and slow to become angry."

– James 1:19

In the hustle of daily life, do you sometimes find yourself talking 'at' your family instead of talking with them? True communication is about more than just words; it's about having listening ears and speaking hearts. This means putting your phone down, actively listening to understand, not just to respond, and speaking in ways that affirm, encourage, and connect.

Consider the approach of Samson, a father of three ranging from a toddler to a teenager, and a devoted husband. He realized early that each family member required a different communication style. With his toddler, he knelt to their level and used simple, clear language. With his school-age child, he fostered open-ended conversations that encouraged expression. With his teen, Samson made sure to be available and approachable, creating a safe space for sharing and understanding. And with his wife, he practiced active listening, showing genuine interest in her thoughts and feelings, and communicated in a way that was both empathetic and supportive.

Samson's strategy was not only about adapting to the developmental stages of his children but also about maintaining a strong, understanding relationship with his wife. He made a conscious effort to listen actively – maintaining eye contact, paraphrasing their words, and showing empathy. This approach opened the lines of communication, making his family feel heard, valued, and understood.

DAD'S DUTY

Today, focus on actively listening to your family members. Whether it's a simple story from your toddler or a complex issue from your teen, give them your full attention. Encourage dialogue that shows understanding and empathy.

PRAYER

Dear God,

Guide me to be a good listener and a thoughtful speaker in my family, fostering open and heartfelt communication that strengthens our bond and understanding.

Amen.

HOMEWORK HELPER AND LIFE COACH

"Teach me good discernment and knowledge, for I believe in your commandments."
— Psalm 119:66

Your involvement in our children's education and growth extends far beyond the classroom. It's not just about helping with homework; it's about being a guiding force in their overall learning journey. This includes both the academic challenges they face and thel life lessons they encounter along the way.

Your role as a homework helper is more than just overseeing school assignments, and providing answers, but about guiding your child through the process of finding solutions. It's an opportunity to instill a love for learning, to encourage problem-solving skills, and to teach the value of perseverance and dedication. It's about supporting them academically while also allowing them to think independently.

As a life coach, your influence extends to teaching them invaluable life lessons — how to deal with failure and success, the importance of persistence, and the value of hard work and dedication. It's about preparing them for the real world, equipping them with the tools they need to navigate life's challenges and opportunities. You play a pivotal role in shaping their understanding of the world, morals, ethics, and life skills.

This holistic approach to your child's education – combining academic support with life coaching – is key to developing well-rounded, confident, and capable individuals.

DAD'S DUTY

Teach your children a basic life skill like sewing a button, organizing a space, or preparing a simple snack. These skills are practical and offer a sense of accomplishment.

_____

_____

_____

_____

_____

_____

PRAYER

Dear God,

Guide me to be both a teacher and mentor to my child, nurturing their mind and spirit in wisdom and understanding, in every aspect of life.

Amen.

> **FATHERHOOD IS NOT SOMETHING PERFECT MEN DO, BUT SOMETHING THAT PERFECTS THE MAN.**
>
> – Frank Pittman

DAD'S DINER: TEACHING THEM TO LOVE FOODS THAT LOVE THEM BACK

45

"So whether you eat or drink or whatever you do, do it all for the glory of God."
– 1 Corinthians 10:31

It's showtime at Dad's Diner! Step into the culinary playground where we're whipping up not just meals, but a love for foods that fuel our bodies and souls.

Educating your children on nutrition isn't just about preparing meals; it's about teaching your children to love and choose foods that nourish and energize them, while encouraging them to only eat unhealthy food and drinks as a treat.

Transforming your kitchen into 'Dad's Diner' can be a fun and engaging way to introduce your family to healthy eating. This involves more than cooking; it includes the process of selecting, preparing, and enjoying healthy foods as well as an enjoyable and educational experience!

You can start by involving your children in meal planning and grocery shopping, turning these tasks into opportunities for learning about nutrition. In the kitchen, involve them in the cooking process. Make it fun by trying out new recipes together, perhaps themed around different cuisines or incorporating a variety of colorful vegetables and fruits.

Through these activities, you're not only teaching your children the importance of healthy eating but also equipping them with valuable life skills. Plus, meals prepared together often taste better and are enjoyed more, making healthy eating a delightful family affair.

DAD'S DUTY

Plan and prepare a meal with your children, focusing on healthy ingredients. Let them help with age-appropriate tasks and explore the fun side of nutrition. Use this time to discuss the benefits of the foods you're using.

_____

_____

_____

PRAYER

Dear God,

Bless our meals and our time together in the kitchen. Guide me in teaching my children the joy and importance of healthy eating for our bodies and spirits.

Amen.

SOLVING THE PUZZLE OF PARENTHOOD 46

"Let your conversation be always full of grace, seasoned with salt, so that you may know how to answer everyone."

– Colossians 4:6

In the Adams family, resolving disagreements was just like solving a complex puzzle. Adam, the dad, often found himself mediating between his two children, Emily and Harry, whose personalities clashed like day and night.

During one dinner, a debate over the family movie night's selection escalated. Emily was set on a comedy, while Harry was adamant about an action flick. As tensions mounted, Adam saw an opportunity for a teachable moment. He acknowledged each child's preference and suggested a creative compromise: a movie-making contest. Emily and Harry would each devise a story blending comedy and action, and the family would collaboratively bring the winning plot to life.

This innovative approach transformed a heated argument into a unifying, creative activity. Excited, Emily and Harry worked together, pooling their ideas. The conflict not only found a resolution but also evolved into an enjoyable family bonding experience, showcasing a homemade movie born from their collective creativity.

Adam's approach demonstrates that parenthood often requires creative solutions to conflicts, emphasizing collaboration and understanding over winning an argument. It's about guiding the family not just through disputes, but towards shared growth and unity.

DAD'S DUTY

Nex time a disagreement arises, try to find a creative and fun solution that involves everyone's input. Use this as an opportunity to teach the value of collaboration and mutual respect.

_____

_____

_____

_____

_____

PRAYER

Dear Lord,

Grant me wisdom and creativity to guide my family through disagreements, turning conflicts into chances for growth, understanding, and unity.

Amen.

GUARDIAN DAD

47

"He will cover you with his feathers, and under his wings you will find refuge; his faithfulness will be your shield and rampart."
– Psalm 91:4

In a world brimming with uncertainties, being a 'Guardian Dad' means more than providing physical safety. It involves guiding your children through life's surprises with wisdom and love.

Your influence extends to everyday situations: from guiding them in handling school pressures, friendships, or understanding the online world. It's about being there for the tough conversations about life's realities, instilling values such as empathy, respect, and perseverance.

You become a moral compass for your children, helping them understand right from wrong, encouraging honesty, and fostering a sense of responsibility. As they encounter life's surprises and obstacles, your steady guidance and unwavering support become their foundation.

Balancing protection with empowerment is key. While you provide a safety net, it's also essential to encourage independence, allowing them to grow, learn, and explore within safe boundaries.

DAD'S DUTY

Create a 'family safety plan' game. Discuss and role-play different scenarios (like getting lost or online safety), allowing your children to suggest actions. This activity educates them on safety while being engaging and interactive.

_____

_____

_____

_____

_____

_____

_____

_____

PRAYER

Dear God,

Help me to be a shield for my family, offering them protection and guidance, while nurturing their strength and independence under Your loving care.

Amen.

WALKING THE TALK WITH THE GOOD BOOK 48

"Let your light so shine before men, that they may see your good works and glorify your Father in heaven."

– Matthew 5:16

Did you know your everyday actions reflect the values you hold and serve as living lessons for your children. It's one thing to teach our children about Christian values, but living them out in our daily lives speaks volumes more than words ever could.

This devotion isn't just about attending church or reading the Bible together; it's about embodying the teachings of Christ in your actions. Whether it's showing kindness to a stranger, honesty in your dealings, forgiveness in your relationships, or patience and love in your family life, these are the moments where your faith becomes tangible to your children.

Your life is a living sermon to your kids. Every act of compassion, every word of truth, every gesture of love and forgiveness is a reflection of your faith and an example for your children to follow.

DAD'S DUTY

Today, involve your children in a 'random act of kindness' activity. It could be anything from writing a thank-you note to someone who's helped you, to doing a small service project together. Let them see faith in action.

_____
_____
_____
_____
_____
_____
_____
_____

PRAYER

Dear God,

Help me to live out Your teachings in my daily life, so my children can learn and grow in faith through my actions and Your grace.

Amen.

MORAL COMPASS FOR THE MODERN DAD 49

"Trust in the Lord with all your heart and lean not on your own understanding; in all your ways submit to him, and he will make your paths straight."
– Proverbs 3:5-6

In today's rapidly changing world, how do you, as a modern dad, steer your children through the maze of moral dilemmas they face? Your role as their moral compass is more crucial than ever. It's about guiding them not just with words, but through the example of your own life and decisions.

The essence of being a moral compass lies in demonstrating values like integrity, empathy, and courage. It involves open conversations about right and wrong, discussing real-life scenarios they might encounter, and exploring these situations through the lens of your faith and moral beliefs.

Your guidance helps them with scenarios like peer pressure, honesty, fairness, and respect for others. It's about helping them understand that every choice has consequences and that making the right choice often requires courage and strength.

DAD'S DUTY

Create a 'Moral Dilemma Game' with hypothetical scenarios. Discuss these situations as a family and explore various solutions, guiding your children to understand the moral implications and the value of making ethical decisions.

_____
_____
_____
_____
_____
_____
_____
_____

PRAYER

Dear God,

Guide me in teaching my children Your ways, helping them to navigate life's moral dilemmas with wisdom, compassion, and a heart aligned with Your will.

Amen.

DOING IT RIGHT, EVEN WHEN IT FEELS WRONG

50

"For we walk by faith, not by sight."
— 2 Corinthians 5:7

Have you ever been plagued with doubt, questioning whether you're making the right choices for your family? Consider the story of Christian, a devoted dad who often found himself wrestling with uncertainty, especially when guiding his teenage son, Isaac, through the challenges of adolescence.

Christian's doubts intensified when Isaac started high school and faced new pressures and decisions. Christian wondered if he was too strict or too lenient, questioning his approach to parenting a teenager. It was during a heart-to-heart conversation one evening that Isaac expressed how Christian's guidance, though sometimes strict, had provided him with a strong moral compass and a sense of security.

This revelation was a turning point for Christian. He realized that his doubts were a reflection of his deep commitment to Isaac's well-being. He learned to trust his instincts and understand that doubt is a natural part of parenting. His experiences taught him that while there are no perfect answers, moving forward with love and faith was the key.

DAD'S DUTY

Write down your recent parenting doubts or challenges. Share these with a trusted friend or fellow dad, discussing how you navigate these doubts. This sharing can be reassuring and provide new perspectives.

_____

_____

_____

_____

_____

_____

_____

_____

PRAYER

Dear God,

In moments of doubt, grant me the wisdom and faith to trust in my journey as a father, guided by Your love and my love for my children.

Amen.

BREAKING THE DAD STEREOTYPES

"Let all that you do be done in love."
— 1 Corinthians 16:14

Being a dad in today's world is more than just being the breadwinner or disciplinarian. It's about embracing a more holistic approach to fatherhood, blending the wisdom of ancient rules with the understanding of modern parenting.

The role of a dad in the family has evolved. Consider the example of a father who swaps traditional roles by taking on the primary caregiver responsibilities while the mother works. This dad actively engages in every aspect of his children's daily lives, from preparing meals to helping with homework, breaking the stereotype of fathers being secondary in domestic and emotional care.

Your involvement can range from participating in their hobbies and interests to having open discussions about life's challenges. It's about being a constant source of love, support, and guidance.

As modern dads, we pave the way for a new understanding of fatherhood - one that values emotional connection, active involvement, and mutual respect. In breaking these stereotypes, we not only enrich our own lives but also set a powerful example for the next generation of fathers.

DAD'S DUTY

Plan an activity based on your child's interests, whether it's a craft project, a sports game, or cooking a meal together. Use this time to connect, share, and learn from each other, breaking traditional roles and enjoying the bond of fatherhood.

_____

_____

_____

_____

_____

_____

_____

_____

PRAYER

Dear God,

Help me to be a father who breaks stereotypes, nurturing and guiding my children with love, presence, and wisdom, and building a strong, loving family bond.

Amen.

STICK WITH IT, DAD 52

"But as for you, be strong and do not give up, for your work will be rewarded."

– 2 Chronicles 15:7

In the rollercoaster ride of fatherhood, have you ever found yourself in moments so challenging that you felt like giving up? These moments test your resilience, but they also offer the greatest opportunities for growth and strength. Remember, perseverance is a key trait of a great dad.

Think back to the sleepless nights with a newborn, the stubborn phases of a toddler, or the rebellious streaks of a teenager. Each phase comes with its unique challenges, and sometimes the pressure can feel overwhelming. It's in these moments that the true strength of a father is shown - not in never struggling, but in choosing to keep going despite the struggles.

Your perseverance is a powerful example to your children. It teaches them about grit, resilience, and the importance of facing challenges head-on. Your determination to stick with it, even when the going gets tough, sets a precedent for them on how to handle life's difficulties.

Carry this truth with you: Your perseverance through adversity is one of the most powerful lessons you can impart to your children. In sticking with it, you're not just enduring; you're teaching, leading, and loving in the most profound way.

Through every challenge and joy, remember: your unwavering love and resilience are the greatest gifts you give as a dad.

DAD'S DUTY

Collect a few stones and decorate them with words or symbols representing strength. Place them around the house as physical reminders of the family's resilience and ability to overcome obstacles.

___

___

___

___

___

___

___

PRAYER

Dear God,

In challenging times, grant me the strength to persevere. Help me to be a steadfast example of resilience and determination for my children, trusting in Your guidance.

Amen.

KEEP THE TORCH ALIVE

Congratulations on reaching the end of this book! I sincerely hope that it has been a valuable companion. As you reflect on the pages you've read, I encourage you to take a moment to pause and contemplate the lessons you've learned, the wisdom you've gained, and the growth you've experienced.

You've journeyed through each page, embracing lessons and insights to elevate your dad game. Now, as you stand equipped to enhance those family bonds, sharpen your parenting skills, balance life like a pro, grow spiritually, and connect with fellow dads, there's one more play to make.

Your thoughts and experiences with this book are invaluable, not just to us but to other dads out there, still searching for their playbook. By sharing your honest review on Amazon, you become a beacon, guiding other dads to the wisdom and support they need.

Think of your review as a high-five to a fellow dad across the globe, a nod of understanding, a gesture that says, "I've been there, and here's something that helped me." Your words can uplift, inspire, and empower.

Leaving a review is simple, yet its impact is profound. It's not just about sharing an opinion; it's about passing on a legacy of knowledge, helping to keep the teachings of God vibrant and alive in the hearts of fathers everywhere.

Here's how you can pass the torch of wisdom:

Scan here to leave a review

Thank you for being a vital part of this journey, for embracing the call to be more than just a dad, and for helping us spread the message of faith, love, and fatherhood. Together, we're not just reading a book; we're nurturing a community, one dad at a time.

Blessings and high-fives,
Your team at Biblical Teachings

www.ingramcontent.com/pod-product-compliance
Lightning Source LLC
Chambersburg PA
CBHW072100110526
44590CB00018B/3246